LOVE 101

A Short Guide to a Long Relationship

Wanda Joy Sylvia

authorHOUSE®

AuthorHouse™
1663 Liberty Drive
Bloomington, IN 47403
www.authorhouse.com
Phone: 1-800-839-8640

Published by AuthorHouse 7/16/2013

ISBN: 978-1-4817-7839-8 (sc)
ISBN: 978-14817-7838-1 (hc)
ISBN: 978-1-4817-7840-4 (e)

Library of Congress Control Number: 2013912563

This book is printed on acid-free paper.

Because of the dynamic nature of the Internet, any web addresses or links contained in this book may have changed since publication and may no longer be valid. The views expressed in this work are solely those of the author and do not necessarily reflect the views of the publisher, and the publisher hereby disclaims any responsibility for them.

To Houston

Gravity is not responsible for people falling in love.

—Albert Einstein

CONTENTS

PREFACE

Let's play a little Family Feud! Ready?
Top three answers are on the board.
Start the clock! *Go!*

Name an activity that anyone in the general public must have a license to do.

Drive a car!
Survey said?
Ding!

Carry a concealed weapon!
Ding!

Get married?
Ding!

Hooray! You win! High fives all around!

You did a *great* job, but please take note of the obvious difference among your three winning answers: driving cars and bearing arms require training, testing, and extensive background checks. Curiously, marriage gets the green light as long as two people can spell their names right. In the interest of public safety, I think we can do better than that.

Last year, while visiting a marriage license bureau for the third time in thirty years, this time in New Orleans, I entertained myself by watching a colorful procession of mates as they entered and exited the license lady's office. When the time finally arrived for my own mate and me to approach, I just had to indulge my curiosity. I sat down and asked the woman, "Do you ever look at a couple and just want to say, 'No. No way. I am *not* giving you a license'?"

She peered up over her glasses, cracked a rare smile, and said, "Yeah, honey, all the time."

So what makes *love* the most contentious subject on the planet? And what on earth would possess a well-balanced person like me to attempt to explain it? The answer, quite simply, is that there is a void—a very big void—possibly more massive than a black hole itself. It might just *be* a black hole, come to think of it. Like you, I have often asked the universe, "Why didn't you give me instructions when I was twenty-one? Where was this data? What about at fourteen, when I *really* needed it?"

The Library of Congress has ten floors dedicated to the many renditions of love. Google it and you'll get eight billion results. You could read them all—or you could read this book. Come on, love can't be that hard. Just like eating, the hard part is actually doing it *right*.

Whether you are about to embark on your first relationship or have had one too many but are brave enough to try it again, please take a deep breath before you rip your heart out and hand it over to the next person. What if the next person *is* your perfect partner? What if this *is* the love of your lifetime? Armed with this book, you will make better decisions and can turn a good relationship into a great one. I would offer you money back on this book, but I know nothing can compensate for a broken heart. I hope this book keeps heartbreak away from you. If this book works for you, please pass it on.

Wanda Joy Sylvia

MY INTRODUCTION
TO LOVE

I was born in Kentucky, the home of many fast women and beautiful horses, on a sparkling Saturday afternoon in late November. There were just two people present at the time of my birth: my mother and me. The delivery was during a shift change, and a transistor radio in the room was broadcasting a college football game in which the twin sons of the obstetrician were playing. With the doctor at the football game, my father away on a business trip, and the nurses clocked out, Mom and I were pretty much left to our own devices. I'm happy to say it all turned out okay.

Though details of my birth seem irrelevant now, the first scratchy sounds that entered my tiny ears—that football game—were very influential. It would take thirty years before my attraction to football players finally faded. Also attractive to me at an early age was the idea of marriage and a family. Possibly influenced by the familial bliss portrayed on shows like *I Love Lucy*, one of my favorite childhood pastimes was thumbing through the layette section of the Sears catalog. In case you are not familiar with these terms, a layette is a collection of baby clothes, and a Sears catalog was a sort of precursor of Wal-Mart. In those days, the Sears catalog was widely known for its lingerie, but its true value to me was the young men's section. All the models looked like college football players—and thus potential husbands.

My first serious romantic proposal came in fifth grade from a boy who had, a few days before, embarrassed the hell out of me by pointing out to the entire fifth grade class that my first bra strap was showing. That may be considered a fashion statement these days, but back then it was scandalous and apparently a covert form of flirting.

At the next morning's breakfast table, I proudly showed my father the faux diamond ring the boy had given me. Father promptly asked to see my amorous suitor, and I retrieved my class photo. After studying it for a moment, father drew a fat yellow pencil from his shirt pocket and marked an *x* over my suitor's face. He then, to my absolute horror, circled the bespectacled face of the class nerd—an undisguised attempt to thwart my youthful love. Thereafter, I kept the ring away from father's sight and nearly rubbed two holes in my class photo trying to erase those pencil marks.

My first kiss that was not directed by a spinning Coca-Cola bottle occurred on the back steps of middle school while waiting on the bus. This event was marked with a heavy yet inexpensive metal bracelet bearing the name of the boy who had kissed me. The metal bracelet was a common method of expressing allegiance to one or another seventh grade boy, as was the far more coveted Saint Christopher medal. Both objects could also serve as trajectory weapons during a common ritual known as breaking up. And, if said bracelet or medal appeared on the appendages of too many girls in sequence, it could be used to exact voodoo-type revenge on the serial offender. Positioning it directly under the leg of a bed, all girls at a sleepover would jump on the mattress as hard as they could. It was then likely that said offender would sustain a non-life-threatening but painful injury at the next football practice.

Common to girls of my era, my first kiss was followed by a series of events referred to as first, second, and third base. These numbers were not necessarily increased with the same person but were merely a convenient way of expressing the level of commitment the girl had to the boy who had instigated the ball game. The vernacular of the time dictated that all boys were "horny" and all girls were either "prudes" or "sluts." The girl's designation depended on a number of factors: socioeconomic status, participation in either cheerleading (with the prudes) or band (with the sluts), and whether or not the girl was involved with an older boy (maximum age difference: three years). The girlfriends of older boys automatically attained slut status regardless of other affiliations. Fortunately for me, I stuck with my own age group.

Due to forces beyond my control, I attended seven high schools in three years—five in southern states and two in Arizona—and went on to attend Vanderbilt University. Actually, I was sent there by my father to avert my stubborn attempt to marry a boy I had met in Arizona. In Arizona I developed a lifelong affinity for hippies, the desert sky, and escapes via my bedroom window in the middle of night. My beau from Arizona would go on to become a Methodist minister. Good thing my father intervened this time—I would never have made a good minister's wife.

My father made rubber bands, which accounted somewhat for my early popularity with the boys. In my twenties, my father suddenly retired, and my family and I found ourselves dreadfully unprepared to carry on his venture. Suddenly finding myself managing a rubber band factory, I retrieved my Vanderbilt business administration textbook from under the philodendron plant, where it had carried out a short but useful task. Almost as suddenly, I found myself married and gave birth to two sons two years apart on the same day. It was around that time that I realized I had potential as an efficiency expert.

You will not be surprised to learn that my first husband (and the father of my sons) was a college football player. He also enjoyed a brief stint as a professional player before reluctantly submitting to the career for which he was destined: high school football coach, a highly revered but seriously underpaid profession. Soon, in order to provide for the life to which I was accustomed, he laid aside his beloved football and took up rubber bands. He was not a reluctant convert to the family business, but neither as rubber band executive nor as my husband was he able to achieve the level of fame he had enjoyed as a football star or even as a coach.

Years passed, my sons grew, the rubber band business expanded— and my first husband grew more inconsolable. So it should come as no surprise to learn that my second husband soon entered the equation. With good character and two children of his own, my second husband seemed to be a suitable role model for my then adolescent sons. What ensued might fairly be characterized as more a debacle than an equation, but in retrospect I prefer to think of it as a learning experience.

After my second husband became my second ex, another predictable event occurred. Just after Y2K, my fortieth birthday, my sons' graduations from high school and departures from home, I gave up my lucrative rubber band career and nearly everything I owned, packed up what I couldn't do without, and moved westward.

I enrolled as a nontraditional (i.e., old) student at the College of Santa Fe. There I met some amazingly brilliant people and a few dumb ones. On the brilliant side was Brother Brian, the black robed master of metaphysics; Dana, the dark mistress of angst poetry; and Philosopher Mark, who explained much to the young students of his fiction workshop in one pithy statement: "Don't you realize that the purpose of your parents is to f—you up?" Things thereafter became much clearer for those troubled youngsters and me.

During my second college experience, I learned another lesson. The college dating scene is *way* different in your forties than in your twenties—in fact, it is, in a word, nonexistent. Any student of similar age was automatically suspect just by being there (why weren't they out sailing the Bahamas?), and the professors were either tenured and frumpy or young and gay. So now where was I to continue my search for the perfect partner? Bars, churches, and yoga classes had already failed me miserably. Home Depot held early promise, but as an apartment dweller I now looked suspicious pushing my empty cart. Then, as the twenty-first century unfolded, the mother lode of matchmaking came on the scene: the Internet.

Suddenly the massive potential of finding someone based upon definable personal criteria was at my fingertips. With a little luck and an eye out for ax murderers and other misfits, I happened upon the love of my life, Z. We quickly connected on many levels and have now enjoyed a decade-long relationship using the steps contained in this book.

Simple rules, guidelines, and supporting exercises make up the steps. Worksheets in the appendix will help you review and reinforce your newfound skills. This book contains time-tested wisdom—not just my own, but also that of my four-person research team, the members of which boast an accumulated 194 years married to the same person . . . not the same same person, but you get the idea.

The guidelines can be interpreted as you see fit. There are two rules, and they are *rules*. We all know rules are made to be broken, but do so at your own peril. It's up to you, but you must agree to one thing: At the first sign of trouble, go back and see what you missed. Once you have tried again and are still absent success, then you can convert this book to cat litter and blame it on me. You are absolutely not to be blamed. But if you have failed to do your homework and follow the steps, then it's your own darned fault.

My one wish for you is simple. May your next relationship be the one to last a lifetime!

CHAPTER 1

U TIME AND WHAT TO DO WITH IT

When you're not sure of what to do, do nothing.
—Dalai Lama

So you think you're ready now, all done with that last mess of a relationship and anxious to get on with it? Not so fast, there, mister or missy. You still have some cleaning up to do. Getting past a defunct relationship and preparing to spend the rest of your life with your perfect partner takes more than just the excavation of that pyramid of Ben & Jerry's containers or beer cans in your living room. This work entails far more than the mere plucking of eyebrows and shaving of legs. (Okay, guys, for some of you, maybe it doesn't.)

The time between committed relationships is an essential time. It is a time to reassess, reaffirm, and rebuild yourself—otherwise known as U TIME. This is the time between, the breathing space, the minute you must give to yourself to get it. What is *it*? *It* is what you really want, your definition of life and of who *you* really are.

U TIME is essential to the strong foundation of a long relationship. An old Indian proverb says, "You can't pour anything into a cup that's full." It may be hard to recognize after a relationship ends, but your cup is positively brimming with wayward emotions and random desires. Perhaps you felt unappreciated. Maybe you felt smothered, or maybe you just couldn't tolerate your in-laws showing up every Saturday night. Whatever caused your relationship to end, U TIME is *the* time for you to identify those issues, pour them out, and avoid wallowing in them ever again.

Now comes a hard truth. An ancient but little known rule of thumb provides a specific amount of U TIME between committed relationships, and my own research consistently validates it. It may seem lengthy, but U TIME is three *months* for every *year* of your last committed relationship. That's right: if your prior relationship lasted one year, you should relax for three months before committing to your next one.

"What?" you whisper, perhaps uttering an expletive or two. What does this author know about my new relationship? She doesn't know about how perfect we are for each other and how in *love* we are!

You are correct, and chances are I never will. However, if a long relationship is really important to you (and I assume that if you are reading this, it is), a three-month-per-year U TIME sabbatical is an essential investment. Statistically, my research shows a strong correlation between a sufficient amount of U TIME and the success of that next relationship. You can probably gauge it yourself by reviewing your friends' and your own experiences. And one added benefit: U TIME virtually eliminates the chance of you calling your new love by the wrong name ever again.

For simplicity's sake, in calculating U TIME, I recommend starting the clock with the first time your former mate tickled your fancy, whatever that means for you, and end with the last time you rolled out of that person's bed. Be honest about it—there's always one last farewell fling. For easy reference, let's call this measure F TIME—the amount of time between first kiss and farewell fling. Be as accurate as you can in your calculations. If you cheat, you only cheat yourself.

For example, if your first date was May 9, 2004, and you had your farewell fling on April 12, 2009, your F TIME is about four years and nine months, or 4.75 years. Then multiply F TIME of 4.75 by three (months for every year) to get a U TIME of 14.25 months, or one year and two months. Okay, round it down to a year if it makes you feel any better.

In simple math, U TIME equals F TIME times .25, or U TIME is F TIME divided by four. Simple, isn't it?

Don't be discouraged. U TIME is simply a time to enjoy and indulge yourself. You can date, make friends, and fool around all you want during U TIME. Hold whatever ritual or exploratory surgery you must to prune away your deadwood and let your heart begin to grow again. But here's the limit. Whatever stage a relationship becomes "serious" to you—be it giving up other romantic interests or sharing the same bench on the subway—you should not "go there" until your U TIME has transpired. Three months for every year—it's a ray of old wisdom that still shines bright today.

But what if you meet the love of your life during U TIME? Then be friends—be the very best of friends. U TIME spent as friends with your future mate is a blue-chip investment in your committed relationship. There is basically only one restriction to U TIME spent with your future mate: if you *do* it, you *blew* it. Repeat it with me: if you *do* it, you *blew* it. If, like me, you consider sex a vital part of the relationship, then you must commit to this. If you *do* it, just stop the clock and start all over again. It's like going directly to jail. Besides, if you are the love of your

3

future mate's life, then he or she will be waiting with open arms (and great libido) when your U TIME is done. If not, you should consider yourself lucky to have avoided a selfish and impatient person—and probably a failed relationship.

There is one exception to U TIME, to all other rules and guidelines—and heck, to this whole danged book. If you are over fifty-five and spent most of your life with the same person and that person has passed away (and you did not cause it), you can close this book right now and give it to Goodwill or someone who needs it. Why? You have already earned your diploma and probably could have written this book. So go out and have fun. Practice serial monogamy. Fly to Vegas and marry somebody. Do whatever you want. Consider it your senior citizen discount.

While the U TIME guideline allows you to safely set an official date for your next serious relationship to begin, there are so many things to enjoy while you wait. You can take up piano lessons or French cooking or yoga or go on that trip to Bali you've always dreamt of. Learn to dine alone and be comfortable with it. Decorate your living space in a style that's all you. Take this time to treat yourself like the king or queen you are, because when that perfect partner comes along, all that precious U TIME will suddenly turn into US TIME.

Besides being extremely good to yourself, there are three exercises to complete during U TIME. The first exercise is to prune away the deadwood of that past relationship. Deadwood consists of things, relationships, and places that are no longer relevant to your newly single status—those things that keep you anchored in the past and prevent you from moving forward. How and how long you should prune depends on several factors. How long did your prior relationship last? How deep was it? How many children resulted? How old are they?

Children change the pruning process entirely. Working together is a close second. If minor children are involved, delicate pruning is mandatory. Remember that the roots of those children run both directions—which, by the way, was at least half your doing. Those roots should be nurtured rather than severed, no matter how hard that may seem at the moment.

If there are no children involved, my pruning advice is to make it as quick, sharp, and painless as possible. Every relationship brings a web of other relationships. Some stick to you (like your kids), and some don't (like your prior mate's college roommate). Your goal is to blow out those loose cobwebs and start fresh, even if it means losing a web or two. If anyone is sticky, he or she isn't going anywhere. Good friends will stick with you, just like your kids. Gooey kids and good friends get to stay. Everything else must go.

The removal of physical reminders is mandatory. You might recall a scene in the movie *Waiting to Exhale* when *Burn*adine piles all her cheating husband's clothing in his BMW and torches it. Then she holds a yard sale to sell his other worldly possessions at one dollar a piece (Honma Clubs and Macallan Scotch included). If you ever find yourself in this situation, seize the day. Grab the lighter, but please abide by local burn restrictions.

Here is a short and handy deadwood-pruning guide.

Clothing: Anything of theirs that you also wore and anything they purchased, unless you picked it out and want to keep it, should be pruned.

Furniture: Prune it unless you picked it out and want to keep it.

Vehicles: Trade these as soon as possible if your ex-mate selected or purchased them. If you also received the payment book, dispose of vehicle at your discretion. If payment book is in your ex-mate's name, consider disposing of that payment book and keeping the vehicle.

Don't forget sporting goods for activities you will never, *ever* participate in again, foods in the pantry or fridge that will never, *ever* pass your lips again, and DVDs, Netflix shows, and TIVO recordings you will never, *ever* watch again.

It's easy to identify the standard items: jewelry, photos, cards, and love letters. If you have children together, give keepsakes to them or store them away for later delivery. My lawyer advises you consult irs.gov for record retention requirements, but if your ex-mate is dumb enough to leave behind vital records, I say . . . *what* records?

Check your devices for texts, e-mails, addresses, and phone numbers. If appropriate, forward them to your lawyer before deleting. Check under the bed and behind the dryer for socks and underwear, in the sofa cushions for gum wrappers and missing jewelry, and under the mattress for magazines. You really won't want to find them later. I have known many people who have replaced their mattresses after a relationship ends, but I am neither strong enough nor wealthy enough for that indulgence and have found that a fresh set of spanking-new thousand-thread-count Egyptian cotton sheets will suffice.

Once the pruning of deadwood is complete, you are ready to advance to the second U TIME exercise: creating your TKT list. There's a form in the appendix to help you get started. TKT stands for "to know thyself," and the goal of the list is to identify the things that are *really* important to you. Narrow them down past the petty stuff, such as thousand-thread-count Egyptian cotton sheets, to the stuff you really *can't* do without—like thousand-thread-count Egyptian cotton sheets. The TKT list is totally personal and totally up to you. It can be as long or short as you like, but it must be thoughtful and thorough.

You can approach your TKT list in a number of ways. I suggest beginning with the basic elements: people, places, things, and events. Try filling in these blanks to get started.

When considering people, try this: "If I landed on a desert island with one *person*, that person would be _____." My advice is to consider

6

personality traits here. If you say Bradley Cooper, you're limiting yourself.

If places speak to your soul, think about this: "If I parachuted out of an airplane like D. B. Cooper, I would want to land in _____."

When things are important, consider this: "If I was a refugee and had to walk four hundred miles to a new home, I would carry _____ with me."

If events motivate you, try this: "If I could spend the rest of my life doing one thing, it would be _____." A few things are automatically ruled out: sex, heroin, and chocolate. Other than that, the field is wide open.

Once you have created and reviewed your TKT list and are happy with it, it's time to commit it to memory. I don't mean just passive memory—I mean deep-down, permanent memory, the kind you use when a cop asks your birth date or airport security asks where you are flying. Think of your TKT list as the password to your soul. It is as important as your mother's maiden name or your daughter's birthday. Also, this immediate-recall ability will save you a lot of fumbling in your pockets when you meet your perfect mate.

Every now and then, check in on your TKT list. Compare it with the real people, places, things, and events in your life. This checkpoint works two ways: first, to see if your TKT list really is what is in your heart and soul, and second, to see if your life is living up to your expectations. Don't be afraid to edit the list. Knowing yourself is quite often an evolutionary process. Sometimes *you* are the evolutionary process. Over time, you should see your TKT list meshing closer and closer with your life. And the more similar the list and your life become, the closer you get to TKT, or enlightenment.

Now armed with your TKT list, you can move on to the third U TIME exercise: PPP—painting the perfect partner. This stage strongly employs the law of attraction. This is not my law but a law common to the universe. I have heard it referred to as the secret, but I don't understand what's so secret about it. It's on Wikipedia.

Here's what Wikipedia has to say about it:

> The law of attraction is the name given to the belief that "like attracts like" and that by focusing on positive or negative thoughts, one can bring about positive or negative results . . . One example used by a proponent of the law of attraction is that if a person opened an envelope expecting to see a bill, then the law of attraction would "confirm" those thoughts and contain a bill when opened. A person who decided to instead expect a cheque might, under the same law, find a cheque instead of a bill.

> Although there are some cases where positive or negative attitudes can produce corresponding results (principally the placebo and nocebo effects), there is no scientific basis to the law of attraction.[1]

I would like to respectfully point out to Wikipedia that prior to 1932, there was no scientific basis for nuclear fission, either. But then some smarty-pants finally figured this out:

$$n(0) + 3Li(6) > 1T(3) + 2He + 4.784 \text{ MeV } (4)$$
$$n(0) + 3Li(7) > 1T(3) + 2He = n(0) - 2.467 \text{MeV}(4)$$

And this was the result:

Now that you get the picture, we can move along to exercise three: painting the perfect partner. This is a fun little exercise. If you are artistically inclined, just whip out your colored pencils and give it a go. There's even a place to create your work of art in the appendix. But if, like me, you can't draw stick figures, you should probably resort to the written word.

As a widely critiqued author of company orientation and training manuals, I have extensive practice in the fine art of do-and-don't lists. The dos are usually no-brainers, like "Clock in on time," "Wear your safety gear," and "Make sure the power switch is in the *on* position before you call maintenance."

Don'ts are often more complex and nuanced. Some are experiential and invoke the situational if/then. For example, "*If* the rubber band formula calls for fifty-eight pounds of rubber, *then* don't throw in a seventy-pound bale just to avoid cutting it." Or "*If* there are flames erupting from your rubber band oven, *then* don't open it."

In painting the perfect partner, the basic dos often get overlooked. These are things like "bathes and flosses regularly," "flushes the toilet," and "chews with mouth closed." It's not until you encounter a partner who *doesn't* uphold the basic dos that you realize they are *must-dos* on your list. Since experience is the best teacher, I will present my first PPP list in reverse. Here's what I know is *not* my perfect partner:

1. wears suits (daily)
2. is overweight or out of shape (this is becoming more loosely defined as years progress)
3. has a routine forty-hour workweek (it's either less than twenty or more than 120)
4. is negative or a worrier
5. lies or cheats
6. is moody, controlling, or mean
7. is an anxious or impatient traveler
8. gossips (yes, men do)
9. is a media junkie (books are an exception.)
10. is egotistical

These are just ten of about 110 characteristics I can now easily identify as things I do *not* want in my mate. There are so many more things that are nuanced, situational, and more elusive to expression in a few short words that I developed a simple exercise to assist in defining them. Again, there's a form in the appendix to get you started. Write a brief on each failed relationship and why you think it failed. Here are two from my own case studies.

Failed Relationship Case #03/98-02/99

Duration: less than one year

Occupation: restaurateur

Physical characteristics: average height, strong build, curly blonde hair

Pros: hippie, adventurer, extensive property owner

Cons: messy house, dirty truck, doting mother

Fault signal number one: partied too much

Rationalization: young—or thought we were

Fault signal number two: long hours at restaurant

Rationalization: fun crowd, good food and drink, wanted to sell it someday

Seminal romantic moment: swimming after hours in the hot water pool at a fine hotel

Intensity: ring at eight months

Living arrangement: separate, mainly his place

Critical fail signals: my avoidance of restaurant events and annoyance when people bought rounds at closing time

Attempted resolution: *the talk* at a Valentine's Day picnic

Result: no picnic—he drove me home and sped away, returning days later to see if I had come to my senses

End of Report

Failed Relationship Case #02/00-01/03

Duration: less than three years

Occupation: sales manager

Physical characteristics: above-average height, average-to-heavy build, clean-cut

Pros: funny, sharp dresser, hard worker

Cons: overly punctual, health issues, aversion to reading

Fault signal number one: showering me with gifts—clothes, jewelry, useless objects

Rationalization: generosity, love

Fault signal number two: growing collection of ostentatious vehicles and Dillard's bags

Rationalization: high income, love of cars

Seminal romantic moment: watching Los Alamos burst into flames from top of Santa Fe mountain

Intensity: ring at two years

Living arrangements: his, then mine

Critical fail signals: collection notices, creditor calls

Attempted resolution: establish budget, work with creditors, have *the talk*

Result: affirmative response to *the talk*, yet within one week a gas-powered miniature Harley Davidson Fat Boy Classic was delivered—it was *soooo* cool

End of Report

By reviewing my don'ts list and compiling my past relationship case studies, I was at last able to develop a positive PPP List. Here are the top ten attributes I wanted in my perfect partner.

1. adventurous and easy traveler
2. creative
3. healthy
4. nature-loving
5. literarily engaged
6. broadminded
7. calm and patient
8. industrious and self-sufficient

9. lucky
10. financially sound

And guess what? The law of attraction worked! With the law on my side and the wonders of modern technology (the Internet), I found Z. Actually, he found me, but that's another story. Z is a colorful person with a very colorful career. He is a professional artist, which is similar in some ways to being a professional gambler. It works like this.

1. You pour your heart and soul out to create the most inspiring, intriguing, and irresistible still objects on the planet.
2. You select a suitable gallery in a locale where people have enough money to purchase your art.
3. You convince the gallery director—sometimes on your knees— that yours are the one and only objects the next patron to walk through the door will be unable to live without.
4. You leave the gallery with a thin piece of paper in exchange for your life's work.
5. You repeat steps one through four, exercising care not to overexpose yourself or oversaturate your market.
6. You check your mailbox day after day after day until one moment in the undetermined future you find an envelope. You rip it open and begin the most fulfilling ritual of an artist's career: the check dance.

This is all perfectly acceptable to Z because he, in his own words, is one of the luckiest men on the planet—not only because he met and married me, but also because he holds a preternatural sense for showing up in the right places. Much like Forrest Gump, Z has found himself sitting in the front row of Saturday Night Live with Art Garfunkel's wife, in Letterman's green room munching chocolate chip cookies with Stedman and Oprah, and sharing a quiet moment with Jack Kevorkian under his laundry line. While Z readily affirms his good fortune, he will also tell you how hard he works to get there. He is one of those industrious people who, when it rains pennies, is out getting pelted in the driving downpour, making sure every bucket in sight is turned right side up.

Our happy home is in Outback, New Mexico, where we garden (okay, sometimes we just try) and make our own beer, wine, cheese, sausage, and fun. We watch the night sky and feed the birds and share a vast library on our e-readers and *love* to get out and travel. So of all the things on my PPP list, I achieved a solid nine out of ten—and as for number ten, I get a little dose of that every time I watch him do the check dance.

Before we move on to chapter 2, here's a quiz to help you review.

U TIME is
   a)   related to the number of Ben & Jerry's containers in your living room.
   b)   reservations at the spa.
   c)   the prescribed amount of time between committed relationships (three months for every year).

Deadwood is
   a)   a town in Arizona.
   b)   a music festival in Northern California.
   c)   the remnants of a past relationship that prevent you from moving forward.

PPP is short for

   a)   Really Gotta Go.

   b)   Personal Pet Peeve.

   c)   Painting the Perfect Partner.

If you answered *c* to all the above, you score an A! Hooray! Now just relax and enjoy your U TIME as you complete your TKT and PPP lists. Just like the flight attendant says, put on your own mask before you assist anyone else. Breathe deep and the oxygen will begin to flow. Soon you will be ready for takeoff!

Chapter 2

Mind the GAP

If you're familiar with this phrase, it will bring to mind that creepy electronic woman's voice you hear just before the doors of a London Underground train smash toward you. If you've never heard the phrase before, you might think you are being commanded to shop for a particular brand of jeans. I use it to make a simple point: people with different life experiences hold different points of reference. I call it the GAP. They see things from a different perspective—or sometimes not at all. This is a good thing, right? I learn from you, and you learn from me.

Minding the GAP is a basic guideline when looking for potential mates. It means identifying and quantifying every basic influence—age, ethnicity, culture, education, economics, politics, or anything that makes you fundamentally who you are and your mate who he or she is. Failure to mind the GAP can result in GAP syndrome: Growing Apart Painfully. Only you and your mate can define your GAPs and decide how critical each GAP is to your relationship. Any GAP can, over a period of close personal contact, become the tie that binds or the one thing that drives you toward homicide.

Obviously, age is a big one and, in most cases, the simplest to identify. In a statistical sense, the vast majority of married couples are two to five years apart in age. Because of that starting point, the vast majority of marriages that "work" follow suit. While many would agree that the age difference can be overcome—"He's so young at heart; "She's a very old soul"—the truth is that as we grew up, we absorbed a huge number of influences that make us the adults (or children) we are. From our youth we bring along values, style, language, tastes, traditions, nostalgia, and, most importantly, memory.

In my case, I have a natural affinity for anyone who remembers when you could only talk on the phone as far away from the wall as the twisted cord would let you, who knows it was once impossible to heat a cup of coffee in under five minutes, and who is today carrying more computing power through airport security than existed on earth at the time of their birth.

In years past, one might argue that ethnicity and culture were as important as age in minding the GAP, but that's no longer the case. Media, technology, and travel have blurred ethnic and cultural lines, and those lines get more faint with every blink of a newborn's eye. While media plays a huge role in blending cultures, it also defines the social values we grew up with (and, like it or not, carry with us). To illustrate, I have compiled this list of popular media for the last seven decades.

Decade	1950s	1960s	1970s	1980s
RomCom	*Honeymooners*	*I Dream of Jeannie*	*Love, American Style*	*The Love Boat*
	I Love Lucy (tie)	*Bewitched* (tie)		
Primary Theme	Guys and girls get married.	Girls are magic (and can create havoc).	Guys and girls fool around.	Grown-ups fool around.
Power Couple	Ozzie and Harriett	George and Jane Jetson	Sonny and Cher	Donald and Ivana
Family Role Model	*Father Knows Best*	*The Addams Family* and *The Munsters* (tie)	*The Brady Bunch*	*Dallas's* The Ewings
Pop Phrases	"They're grrreat!"	"Nothing sucks like an Electrolux."	"Have it your way."	"Like a rock."
		"Does she or doesn't she?"	"Try it— you'll like it."	"This is your brain on drugs."
		"If it feels good, do it."	"The devil made me do it."	"Where's the beef?"
Game Show	*Truth or Consequences*	*The Newlywed Game*	*Family Feud*	*Wheel of Fortune*

Decade	1990s	2000s	2010s
RomCom	*Friends*	*Sex and the City*	*Girls*
Theme	Guys and girls have fun.	Guys and girls have sex.	Guys and girls are awkward.
Power Couple	Marge and Homer	Ozzie and Sharon	Brangelina
Family Role Model	*Married with Children's* the Bundys	The Bluths	The father from *Sh*t My Dad Says*
Pop Phrases	"Once you pop, you just can't stop."	"What happens here stays here."	"There are some things money can't buy."
	"It's everywhere you want to be."	"Keeps on going and going and going."	"Can you hear me now?"
	"Just do it."	"I'm lovin' it."	"ROTFLMAO"
Game Show	*Who Wants to Be a Millionaire?*	*Deal or No Deal*	*Survivor*

Now let's look at two cases of a well-known exception to the age gap: the May-September romance. This one I hold some personal knowledge of. You see, my father was fifty-three and my mother was twenty-one when they married. In other words, he was thirty-two years old when she was born. As a rubber band maker, he obviously had a knack for stretching things. And my mother obviously had dreams other than mountain biking and running marathons together when she married him. But she was reportedly very much in love with him, and he thought she was the most beautiful woman (read: *girl*) in the world.

They had just celebrated their fortieth wedding anniversary when he passed away. He had given her four beautiful children, me being number three when he was sixty-six, and my younger sister when he was seventy. Apparently he was a virile old chap, but no doubt it helped a lot that she was young and beautiful. From an insider's perspective, they had a fairly happy relationship that went like this: he did what he wanted and she did what he wanted. The trouble didn't seem to start (for her) until one fateful day when he came home from work and announced his retirement, on that day, at age eighty-eight. As I recall, his exact words were "I'm not going back to the office again."

He then proceeded to become what he was: a *very* old man. He also became a far more jovial and patient man, but that's another book altogether. The trouble with this gap was that my mother, who was about my current age at the time and, also like me, still attractive, was thrust from being the trophy bride of a successful businessman into being caretaker for an old fart. She did this with her typical grace and aplomb, but I could tell deep down that she had to work on it. I believe she did enjoy the newfound freedom that came with being the head of the household and the main signatory on the bank accounts, but somehow that seemed insignificant to the task at hand.

For the next six years, she took very good care of him, and he was very grateful. Yet when he died, another effect of the gap presented itself: my mother became a fairly young widow. Here she had matured with this man as master and commander, and now she was adrift at sea. She partook in the normal mourning period, but instead of picking herself up, dusting her pretty old self off, and heading out to find her next captain, she settled into the life of a lone sailor. My siblings and I chided her and prodded her and even tried to set her up with a fellow or two, to which she always replied, "Your father would be such a hard act to follow." Though my parents had a statistically successful marriage, my mother is nearing ninety and has lived almost seven decades with a GAP she never closed.

Conversely, I have a dear friend who married a man almost fifteen years her junior. To further challenge herself, she is a US citizen, and he a born-and-bred German. The relationship started most romantically. She was on a beach vacation with her mother and sisters and he, attending film school nearby, was there to have some fun with his buddies. Obviously his plan was a major success. Their crossed paths led to many a late night under the moonlight exploring the texture of sands along the Gulf of Mexico. When vacation time ended, they continued a lovely long-distance relationship for several years until he completed his degree.

The wedding, likewise, was lovely, this time with sand under just their toes and the sweet ocean breeze affirming their devoted promises. She relocated to his world for several years, and then he relocated to hers. She learned German and loved his German family, while he heartily embraced her American ways. He was a budding filmmaker and avid chef, and she was a working professional who devoured his gourmet meals after long days at the office. They travelled together, read together, fixed up their home together, and, as he was a film buff, watched every movie ever made.

It all appeared quite lovely, until one day it wasn't. She ran into an old boyfriend and, in a fit of lust, ran away with the man, leaving her poor German boy with all the time in the world for his movies. I never quite figured out if it was the age difference, nationality, culture, or economics that broke them. Perhaps it was all those movies. I remember her referring to them as her seven-dollar naps. Regardless, the GAP swallowed them. Perhaps they could have minded it more.

Minding the GAP does not mean the GAP is nonnegotiable. First you should identify it and honestly try to assess whether it will swallow you whole or can be bridged. With my husband, Z, there is one GAP that we negotiate daily. While I was never raised to believe that I "came from money"—my father was a tightwad, and my mother a Depression-era baby—there was never a question as to where my next meal would come from or whether I would have new school shoes. In contrast, Z came from a strictly working-class family in a depressed town at a time when neighborhoods were being burned in race riots.

Child labor in the family was still acceptable in "our day," but mine consisted of fifty-pound gunnysacks of scrap rubber bands that I would pile in the yard and invite my friends over to sort through for the good ones. It was like a big Easter egg hunt. All in all, we earned about twenty cents an hour, but it made us feel so accomplished—and rich!

In contrast, Z's childhood labor was provided by his uncle Roger, who would pull up at the corner of Pleasant and Hazard Streets, tell Z to jump in his van, and drop him off at an abandoned warehouse with instructions to rip out all the copper pipe. Then Uncle Roger would speed away. A few hours later, Uncle Roger reappeared, threw open the van doors, piled in all the copper pipe the van would hold, threw Z a twenty-dollar bill, and sped away again, leaving Z with a feeling of great accomplishment but no ride home.

Now, as a child, Z made a lot more money than I did, but that's not the point here. The point is that Z's twenty dollars might have been used to buy his school shoes or put a meal on the table, while mine was just candy money with little more significance than a Monopoly buck. The result is that Z absolutely *loathes* letting anything—and, I repeat, *anything*—go to waste.

As a professional artist, Z earns a good living from his talents, so money is not the issue here. The issue is that he hoards everything and anything that could somehow be reused, recycled, or repaired. He once had a successful run of making "found object" sculptural art—intriguing reincarnations of rusted shovels, box springs, and transmission parts. As a result, people began to bring him treasures—truckload after truckload that piled up into high-rise apartments for all the varmints of the desert. Fortunately for me, those apartments are on a remote piece of property nowhere near our home, but I know someday we must deal with them. Even if he welds and sculpts and enjoys a major uptick in the found object art market for the rest of his life, he will *never* use up all his treasures.

Our garage is a source of major contention. To me, it is a public space where tools and supplies are stored in an organized fashion to be used by anyone on the property with the requirement that the objects be replaced in a timely fashion to their proper designated spots.

To Z, the garage is sacred ground, a temple where only Z, with his magical all-seeing rewind memory, can recall the exact location of a number-eight pentalobular hex key as long as *he* is the only being on earth who has touched it. As he has reminded me more than a million times, "If you move it, you might as well throw it away." I once saw him sniffing the handle of a crescent wrench just to see if it held my scent.

To keep my hands off his tools, Z has even bought me my own "toolbox," an adorable collection of Chinese-made gadgets that is just short of having *Barbie* printed on top and being made completely from plastic. My reaction on the few occasions when I actually attempted to *do* something with these gadgets cannot be printed in a publication without a brown paper wrapper.

Often I resort to the dark of night to "borrow" a flathead screwdriver from the garage and engage in the dangerous act of changing a light switch cover. (Yes, I do it with the light on. I know it's dangerous, but it must be done.) I admit, when I'm feeling unusually brave and/or frustrated, I do sneak in and organize certain parts of the garage just for the therapeutic value. But I know I am taking my life in my own hands. Usually, within a few hours, I will hear a series of bangs and crashes to signal that Z has discovered my therapy session. By then, I am feeling much better and can resist the temptation to stroll by the garage and say, "Hey, honey, what's up?"

As you may know, my tenure in running a rubber band factory has left me an efficiency expert. I am highly trained at 5S, Kaizen, TPS, JIT, Kan-Ban, and Poka Yoke. When it comes to organizing things, I halt just short of jujitsu. Yet the only talent I have been able to bring from these years of experience to *our* garage is the Japanese heijunka box—as in pile everything that is outdated, overused, or just plain broken in a box and label it "Hey, Junk Box!" Okay, I have been nice and labeled these boxes "For Art?"

So, how do Z and I resolve this GAP? Well, for one, we do a slow dance I like to think of as treaty negotiations. He has a large studio, and I have vowed never, not ever, in no way on any day to touch anything in it—not even to take out the trash. If I find him lying dead on the floor, I suppose I could move him then, but I'd still have broken my vow. I am so committed to this that I knock before entering his studio, getting permission first before I move his airspace, and he then answers "Who's there?"—even though we are often the only people within twenty miles.

For his part, Z is beginning to understand the value of storage space and how technology can make us more efficient. For example, moving four cases of old *Arizona Highways* magazines for the last two decades just so you can retrieve that perfect photograph of a 1954 Rambler against a desert sunset when you feel inspired to paint it has now been replaced by Google Images. Internet shopping has completely eradicated the need for outbackers like us to move and store two containers containing roughly *eighty-four* recycled duplex electrical sockets just in case we have to replace *one* someday.

Don't get me wrong—I am a solid advocate of recycling and reusing and would never waste or throw out things needlessly. For the most part, I would rather visit the dentist than stand in line at the hardware store. But after years of arranging and rearranging my goods through various incarnations of my life, I have a fairly good grasp on what I can and can't do without. And Z is beginning to get the idea. I even found some *Arizona Highway* magazines in the trash bin the other day. Don't tell him, but I pulled out three and hid them under the mattress. I know I'll find time to read them . . . someday.

So before we move ahead to the first *rule* of *Love 101*, let's take a minute to review the GAP and how to mind it. The first step in minding the GAP is to identify and acknowledge the major GAPs between you and your mate. Knowing your GAPs ensures a more clear-headed approach to a developing relationship, particularly with other strong forces (read: *lust*) at play. Armed with awareness of your GAPs, future conversations (read: *arguments*) can move from "Why are you are so darned _____?!" to "I understand that you are _____, but . . ." Marriage counselors count this as a major shift in the right direction.

Second, assess those gaps as honestly as you possibly can. Do you think they can be bridged, or could they potentially grow into the Grand Canyon? Assessing them early will prepare you and your mate for the moment you encounter them. And, if you are around each other long enough, you surely will. Mind you, minding the GAP is not about passing judgment. It is about paving the smoothest road possible for a long and thriving relationship.

CHAPTER 3

THE THREE-YEAR RULE

To really know someone is to have loved and hated him in turn.
—Marcel Jouhandeau

In college, Professor Dana, the dark mistress of angst poetry, had an unnerving high-pitched cackle she would emit just after assigning a particular exercise to our intermediate poetry workshop. She called it the Nazi Tactic. The Nazi Tactic involved pouring your heart out on a piece of paper to create the most moving, soul-wrenching, life-changing sequence of alliterated, rhythmic, and soothing words ever to exist on the planet. Then you must analyze, edit, carve, cut, shave, and rearrange these words until they became at once emboldened and enlightened. You must consider the placement of every letter, every option for every adverb, whether each of the *the*s should be a *the* or should alternately be an *a* . . . or perhaps a *that* or perhaps nothing at all.

Then you must bring your finished piece of literary art to said intermediate poetry workshop (a.k.a. Dana's Dungeon), where she would remain pensive and silent while your own voice cracked as you recited it in front of her and a dozen postpubescent boys and girls (your peer group). Then said peer group was encouraged to taunt, skewer, rip apart piece by piece, and eventually slay your creation before your very eyes. Then—and this is where the fun comes in—you had to go home, choose just one most precious line of your verbal creation to save, and start all over again.

Where am I going with this? If you must leave everything else in this book behind, take this one rule with you—the Three-Year Rule. If you take one and only one lesson from these pages, this is the one worth saving.

It is a rule with serious reason, and can only be sidestepped if you are using your senior citizen discount—with, possibly, one other exception, which I will explain soon enough. (Patience is a key part of the lesson here.) The Three-Year Rule is simple but firm. You should wait *three years* after beginning a serious relationship (whatever that means to you) before you set that relationship in stone.

Right now you may be thinking, *Yeah, more like three centuries.* But it's really not. Three years is probably not much more than a blip in the big picture of the rest of your life. It's less than high school and less time than it took to learn to tie your shoes. Plus, you will know your mate three years better. Three is my documented number of years it takes for Prince William to turn into Don Draper and then go on to assume the personality of Hannibal Lecter. These are things you simply need to know before you legally commit to waking up to someone every morning.

In the olden days, "set in stone" meant setting a stone in your wedding rings. Today that step is often skipped before commingling genetics and/or assets. So wait three years before you set it in stone— whatever that means to you. That's the Three-Year Rule. *But,* you're thinking, *we're in love* right now *and must get on with it! Hurry! What's that exception to this silly Three-Year Rule?* Patience, grasshopper—you will learn soon enough.

Now that you know what the Three-Year Rule is, let's look into what happens during those three critical years of early relationship, beginning with what love is and why we fall in it. Here's what our pal Wikipedia has to say.

> Falling in love is mainly a Western concept of moving from a feeling of neutrality towards a person to one of love. The use of the term "fall" implies that the process is in some way inevitable, uncontrollable, risky, irreversible, and that it puts the lover in a state of vulnerability, in the same way the word "fall" is used in the phrase "to fall ill" or "to fall into a trap". The term is generally used to describe an (eventual) love that is strong.[2]

That strong love—that's the one we're after, right? But according to the fields of psychology, physiology, and biology, there is no fast track, only three indisputable stages. One must graduate through two stages—lust and romance—before arriving at the desired stage of "strong" commitment.

Before we look at how these stages progress, I would like to pause to exclude something from our conversation: lust for lust's sake, often called "sport sex." The late John Money, a noted sexologist and professor of medical psychology at John Hopkins University, made this distinction: "Love exists above the belt, lust below."[3] Dr. Money was obviously somewhat limited in perception, or he would have acknowledged that lust could also exist above the neck (i.e., in the mind) and, at its best, often does so. Now, I do not mean to discount lust. Historically, it is responsible for most of the life on the planet. Every postpubescent being with a heartbeat understands it. Still, lust for lust's sake is excluded from this conversation.

Now let's proceed. According to research by Lisa Diamond, a developmental psychology professor at the University of Utah, lust and romance are driven by different underlying forces. Lust evolved for the purpose of sexual mating (to produce more humans), while romance evolved to support infant bonding (to prevent us from eating our young.)[4] While both are essential to human life on the planet, each mixes a unique cocktail with different results.

As for lust, we can credit that mostly to estrogen and testosterone, those old friends we got to know at about the same age we discovered our young bodies were capable of some interesting new tricks. Estrogen and testosterone take full credit for those tricks, as well as for the new set of gadgets that suddenly appeared to perform them. Little estrogen and testosterone seemed rather fun and harmless at that young age, but when nurtured to their full potential, they can exceed the power of nuclear fission. Just ask any menopausal woman. And scientists observe that they possess roughly the addictive powers of heroin. Now *that's* attraction.

Past lust, we find another highly pleasurable stage: romance. Aah— when you can scarcely inhale but to detect the scent of your beloved, when every letter on every billboard spells out their name, when every love song ever composed is just about the two of you, when every step you take leads you back together again. Oh, for the love of romance!

I hate to pop that lovely pink bubble you're floating in, but romance is primarily a chemical reaction too. At least three more chemicals find their way into the massacre of the heart during this stage. The flush of skin and loss of rationality that meet your mate's alluring smile is really overabundant dopamine, a pleasure-seeking chemical; its racy sister norepinephrine, responsible for making your heart race;

and phenylethylamine, which is found in psychedelics, chocolate, and amphetamines. Legally, this cocktail should come with a disclaimer like "May cause excessive loss of hair, appetite, and sleep. Consult your physician if you experience thoughts of suicide or an erection that lasts over four hours." But nobody has yet found a way to post a disclaimer on romance. In fact, the Family Lawyers Association is primarily responsible for its absence.

The most important thing that you can't possibly be aware of in the romance stage is that you will, in fact, excessively idealize your love. The old saying "love is blind" captures the essence here. That massive amount of chemicals your body is releasing just now will not only cause sleeplessness and possibly a prolonged erection, but will also inhibit your natural production of serotonin. Who needs serotonin, you ask? Well, you do. It is the chemical that encourages you to apply a balanced assessment to situations. It is the magic juju that, when missing, leads to obsessive-compulsive disorder, or OCD. Are you a bit OCD about your mate? You might want to check your serotonin levels.

Note that, without serotonin, not only will you obsess over this new mate of yours, but your whole world will suddenly shine brighter and more beautiful than ever as well. You will suddenly smile at the grouchy, stinky people on your commuter train. You will laugh when a large SUV cuts the curb and projects a mud puddle over your entire pedestrian person. You will actually try to engage the next telemarketer in a meaningful conversation. Wait, what? Yes, you will. You are in love! How sweet it is! Who *wouldn't* want to be addicted to this?

So please go on. Enjoy it to its fullest. But also please note that you are under the extended influence of a highly potent and almost bottomless cocktail for which there is no Breathalyzer test that can take away your keys. And, thanks to the Family Lawyers Association, there are no warning labels, either.

Okay, so now that I have taken all the romance out of love and replaced it with chemistry, let me go on to say that if the romance is strong and felt by both of you, it will progress to the third stage: commitment. With commitment come some quirky chemicals to really mix up your love potion. When that seminal moment arrives that you throw caution to the wind and melt in rapture into each other's bodies, everything changes. Sex is a turning point.

Duh, you think. *Did I buy this book just to find that out? Come on, what is that exception to the Three-Year Rule?*

Patience, grasshopper.

The change we are now discussing is brought about by (the act of) sex. It is strictly scientific and is unrelated to your mate now having a key to your apartment. When you have sex, your body produces another set of chemicals. Notable among these are oxytocin and vasopressin. These little jewels are responsible for that warm, fuzzy rush you feel as you lay back on your pillow and light that cigarette. Oh, wait—that's so thirty years ago. I suppose now you check your text messages.

Fortunately, the chemicals produced by sex are also responsible for that feeling of well-being and bonding that allows you to remain in each other's arms long after your left hand has gone completely numb. The more sex you have, the more these chemicals are released, and the more bonding occurs. Did I just say that sex leads to commitment? I think so—or at least that's what occurs chemically. On the other hand, I suppose it could lead to a serious guilt trip.

With sex and its related abundance of oxytocin and vasopressin, here is where the havoc comes to call. Studies show that—much like a mother-in-law—high levels of oxytocin and vasopressin actually block dopamine and norepinephrine pathways. And when pleasure-seeking dopamine and her heart-racing sister norepinephrine get stopped in *those* high heels, let me tell you—trouble is a-brewin'.

Dopamine deficiencies are known to cause social withdrawal, apathy, attention deficit, and the inability to experience pleasure. So, after months of awesome romps in the sack, you awake one morning to see that your giant hunk of steaming passion has left a giant heap of stinking socks right in the path to the bathroom. Fortunately, if your oxytocin and vasopressin are strong enough, you will now be well into the committed stage and give that heap a numb yet loving smile just before you kick it out of the way—the socks, that is, not the mate. When you have done that, you are truly enjoying a long relationship. And that's what we're after here, right?

So there they are, the simple facts. You begin with lust, then graduate to romance, and end up committed. Or, in the chemical version, you begin with estrogen and testosterone, graduate to dopamine and norepinephrine, and end up on oxytocin and vasopressin. I don't know about you, but that sure sounds like drug addiction to me.

I believe the old folks tried to tell us, "Marry in haste, repent at leisure," but old folks have routinely been ignored for eons. Fortunately for us, we now have ample research data to support their silly folklore. For example, Larry Young of the Yerkes National Primate Research Center at Emory University has spent a substantial amount of time and money studying the prairie vole, one of only 3 percent of mammals (besides humans) that are predisposed to "mate for life."[5]

Mated prairie voles even avoid other voles of the opposite sex, though Larry has not yet determined whether or not vole mates are actually capable of a jealous rage. Mated prairie voles work together to care for their young and spend hours grooming and hanging out with each other, which sounds to me like the perfect long relationship.

Larry set out to determine why the prairie vole is capable of this very special long relationship, while its close relative, the montane vole, just runs around like the animal it is, hooking up with every hottie vole that crosses its path. He found that, like humans, when voles have sex, oxytocin and vasopressin are released.

The difference between prairie and the montane voles is that the prairie vole has the necessary receptors to experience the bonding effects of oxytocin and vasopressin, while the montane vole does not. Thus the prairie vole experiences what commitment is, while the montane vole just goes on sport-sexing it up. You can probably relate this to some humans you know, but please refrain from calling them voles. They might take offense. The voles, that is.

Applying the same level of curiosity to humans, Ted Huston, a professor of human ecology at University of Texas, conducted a fourteen-year study of 168 male and female couples.[6] In his extensive study, he found two conclusions to support the Three-Year Rule:

1. The longer the courtship, the stronger the long-term relationship.
2. Successful relationships are slow and steady and unfold over time.

I can advance Dr. Huston's findings by light-years with one simple fact. In the course of human events, the longer the time span, the more s—hits the fan. All chemistry, psychology, and primate studies shoved aside, the real reason for the Three-Year Rule is this.

It is statistically impossible to encounter any three-year span in your life that does not include at least

- one financial crisis,
- one family crisis,
- one friend crisis,
- one physical crisis (car accident, theft, house fire, etc.), and

- cumulative lesser dramas, such as a simultaneous dripping faucet, clogged drain, and declined credit card when you try to pay the plumber.

Over the course of three years, you will endure a span of time during which almost everything that could possibly go wrong in you or your mate's life will do so. If you have weathered them together, you will know how that person holds up. You will see their true character. You will see if they cut and run, sull up and stew like a prune, or stand tall and walk through that wall of fire with you.

You will also see how many crises and dramas your potential mate can attract during that three-year period. If that number is severely greater than yours, then you should be the one to cut and run.

To further support the Three-Year Rule, I offer you this. Almost anyone can put on a good front for a period of time, but no one, and I mean *no one*, can pull it off for a solid three-year run. I don't care how good an actor you are or how many Academy Awards you have won. Even Liz Taylor proved eight times that it couldn't be done.

And if it is you doing the acting—all lovey-dovey and happy like you enjoy a daily poke in the eye—the Three-Year Rule applies to you too. Sometime around that three-year mark you will wake up one day, take off that muzzle, and start slobbering and biting like hell. Yes, rabid dogs behave better. I'm not trying to be ugly here; I'm just speaking from a position of personal knowledge.

Between Z and me, we have forty-one years of marriage, although only one year of that arrangement has been spent married to each other. Just to be sure that the marriage would stick this time, we preceded it by adhering to the Three-Year Rule not once, but three times in a row. As a result, I believe I can say that this is the first time I recited that "death do us part" thing and actually thought I could achieve it.

So that's it—the Three-Year Rule. *But wait!* you're thinking. *What about the exception???* Oooohhhhkaaaay, you've stuck around this long. Here it is . . . but you must pay close attention . . . even closer than you paid to the Three-Year Rule.

The exception requires an extended trip abroad together—and I don't mean a ten-day cruise or a cottage in the French countryside. If the two of you can endure an extended overseas trip together—a month or more, preferably in a third-world country—and *if* you weather it without *one single* spat or cross word, then go ahead and commit. Congratulations, you have found that rare jewel of a relationship. But remember: *no spats.*

I don't know exactly what it is—jet lag, strange sights and smells, getting shoved like a sardine into a train car between unidentifiable creatures (some of whom might be human)—but extended travel abroad brings out the elemental character in all of us, no matter what the chemistry. If you can avoid massive local libations and observe your mate, you will quickly see the impact of this thrown-to-the-wolves experiment. You will see what they are truly made of. But you must pay *close* attention. If there's evidence of even the slightest hint of failure mode, you must *immediately* revert to the Three-Year Rule.

Before I married for the first time, I actually had the opportunity to experience this travel-abroad exception. A few months into that relationship, my first future husband and I went on a six-week tour of Europe for the purpose of (I am not making this up) industrial rubber band espionage. That's right. At the direction of a slightly psychotic business associate, we were sent off to assume false identities and make our way past tight security forces into the inner chambers of Europe's rubber band factories.

Besides learning more about European rubber bands than would ever prove practical, I also learned quite a lot about my mate, much of which I do not wish to recall to this day. To briefly summarize, a few weeks into our mission, I swore that when my feet touched American soil again, I would get down and kiss it—and then kiss him good-bye and never, ever so much as speak his name again.

It would be fourteen years before that relationship ended. But being so young and inexperienced at the time—and lacking a copy of this book—everything returned to relative normal once we returned home. Instead of kissing good-bye, we kissed and made up and got married within three months. Looking back, I could have saved so much time and anguish had I just paid attention to that one moment in a German train station when he sent one of my seven pieces of luggage flying across the old tile floor. But I did learn one lesson: pack light.

This travel-abroad exception might be a bit expensive, but if you're in such a darned rush, consider it the expedited service. Just be sure to pay attention to what you're about to learn on this bullet train ride. I have to emphasize that this may fast-track you past the Three-Year Rule, but it may not.

If there are any signs of failure, no matter how small, you must revert to the Three-Year Rule. There is no other way around it. Just sit back, relax, and enjoy what could turn out to be the best three years of your life. What do you have to lose—except a little time?

CHAPTER 4

DEAL OR NO DEAL

Within the first five minutes of meeting someone, you
will know the reason that you will leave them.
—*Anonymous*

In every long relationship, negotiations are ever present, both with your mate and within yourself. Some things, like my next example, are easy deal breakers, and some take longer to prove themselves. Also, some might surprise you and turn out, in the long run, not to be deal breakers at all. It's all in the negotiations.

The most identifiable deal breaker I ever encountered came from a question I hadn't asked and thus hadn't answered. During my early experimentation with the then new phenomenon of online match making, I found a cutting-edge service that determined your perfect match based on an extensive emotional, intellectual, and socioeconomic profile.

What could be better, I thought, than doing away with the guesswork and letting a computer figure it out for you? I anxiously enrolled and set about completing the three-plus hours of personal inquisition that the service required, the final question of which entailed my geographic boundaries to find a potential soul mate. After all that work, my obvious answer was *anywhere* in the world.

And off it went with its host of logical algorithms and intimate information in search of my most perfect match in the world. After a day or two of data crunching, the service came back with one and only one match—and he happened to be on the exotic island of Maui. Oh, be still, my beating heart! How perfect could it get?!

Immediately I engaged in an e-mail dialogue with Maui Mr. Right and learned we had much in common. He was a divorcé with two grown sons—so was I. He was an heir to a business who felt chained by the "golden handcuffs"—so was I! He was a hippie child who wanted a utopian lifestyle and peace on the planet—*so did I!*

When it came time to meet, I boarded the plane in Dallas with a nervous stomach and touched down in Maui with so much gastronomic distress I was the last person to disembark. As I finally descended the escalator toward the arrivals lounge, I saw my potential paramour waiting anxiously at the bottom of the stairs, lei of ilima flowers in hand, bronzed face aglow in the afternoon light.

For a moment I felt like I was floating on the stairway to heaven. He was even more attractive than his photos had whispered, his warm eyes twinkling and his smile beckoning me closer. Yet as I approached my one and only match in the whole wide world, I experienced an Alice in Wonderland moment: I felt myself growing taller and taller while he shrank and shrank.

The moment we met eye to eye, I at 5'7" and he every bit of 4'10" on his toes, we both realized the critical GAP that our high-tech matchmakers had failed to mind: the one of height. And the look on his face told me it was every bit as important to him as it was to me.

So while we enjoyed a friendly dinner that evening, it was quite obvious there was nowhere else to go. We had—toe-to-toe, but definitely not eye to eye—encountered a nine-inch deal breaker.

Even despite your best attempts to manifest a fully loaded PPP list, you will encounter deal/no-deal decisions daily. And you will allow some no-deals to squeak by based on (1) severity, (2) frequency, and (3) likelihood of change. Chemistry can also make no-deals look and feel like real-deals for months or even years, depending on the frequency of lovemaking and other forces. Yet the more no-deals you let pass as deals, the higher the odds that one morning you will awake to a deal breaker (often called taking off the rose-colored glasses).

Watch for specific things in your TKT list and changes in your dress, social activities, or people in your life. For most of my life, I had a big closet and could gauge the length of a relationship by measuring the distance the clothes of that relationship took up on my closet bar. When I finally learned to stick to my favorite—T-shirts and cutoffs—I no longer needed the bar or the closet.

You might find yourself suddenly hanging out with a type of people different from what you're used to. I'm not talking race, color, or even class—just general type. Type can be gauged by many indicators, from the type of vehicles in the driveway at social functions to the number of teeth. If you're uncertain, you can float a few buzzwords from your common vernacular out at the holiday dinner table to see what happens.

For example, I once used the term "Dow Jones" as I passed the gravy bowl. After a few moments of silence, a great stir erupted around the table. Apparently sometime ago, a poor fool named Dow had left his loving wife Mary Lou and their three little ones to run off with that known floozy Lavonda. Unfortunately I had to excuse myself to clean the gravy from my lap and never learned whether the poor fool's last name was really Jones.

And while I'm all for trying different social activities, if on more than one twenty-eight-degree morning you find yourself wishing for latte and croissant while dragging a deer carcass down the side of a mountain, you've probably gone too far. Yet even this situation can be turned into a non-deal breaker if you abide by the TKT guideline and, instead of acting like you love the deer woods, spend that time doing what *you* truly love to do. And do not lord it over anyone. The best way to make a deal out of a deal-breaking event is to allow your mate to enjoy it, whatever it is, *without* guilt and *without* you.

The operative word in negotiating deals is *compromise*. Every negotiation is give-and-take, and every relationship is a series of negotiations. My 194-year research team puts it like this. If one person is 75 percent of a relationship, the other is 25 percent, and they both consider themselves to be the 75 percent, then it's a win-win. That's the *real deal*.

CHAPTER 5

GIRLS ARE SILLY, AND GUYS ARE DUMB

This very simple guideline is often referred to as the gender gap. Its more colorful form—Silly and Dumb—was contributed to my studies by Z himself. I have thought deeply on it since he pointed it out a decade ago, and I have to say that I think he's right. All anyone really need do to validate it is visit a playground. Note the girls giggling and fluttering around the swing sets and the boys yodeling and plunging head first from the top of the jungle gym.

The main difference, of course, boils down to three little letters: s e x. Wikipedia gives *sex* the high honor of calling it a *disambiguation*. That means it holds a number of definitions. In the case of sex, it holds a record nine. They are as follows:

- Sex, the biological distinction between male and female . . .
- Sexing, the act of discerning the sex of an animal
- Sexual reproduction, a process of combining and mixing genetic traits, associated with the generation of new individuals . . .
- Animal sexual behavior

- Human sexual activity
- Sexual intercourse . . .
- Non-penetrative sex, or sexual outercourse
- Gender, the social distinction between male and female
- Human sexuality[7]

In his best-selling book *Men Are from Mars, Women Are from Venus*, relationship expert John Gray puts an otherworldly spin on the gender gap, proposing that gender differences are really a matter of universal order. I, however, find gender differences more earthly defined as "silly" and "dumb." To support my findings, I contrast a few common colloquialisms used by the sexes for that one simple word: *sex*.

Girls: *bed*; guys: *bang*
Girls: *sleep with*; guys: *score, home run*
Girls: *be intimate*; guys: *give it up*
Girls: *you know*; guys: *hizzit the skizzins* (Okay, guys, you got me on this one. I really *don't* know.)

Unless you are gay, in which case you can probably skip this chapter entirely, you'll encounter the gender gap on a daily basis. But because most of us are so familiar with this gap, it rarely reaches deal-breaker levels. Most gender gaps hold simple resolutions. If it weren't that way, we would have given up and just resorted to more gender-friendly relations long ago. But then, life on the planet must go on.

Spanning gender gaps is often as simple as "Yes, dear" or a vacant "Uh-huh" and a quick peck on the forehead. Much like congress, you eventually learn that it takes awhile to reach across the aisle. Now that Z and I have returned to relatively normal chemical levels, we encounter more and more gender gaps every day. Here are a few along with our (so far) time-tested resolutions.

GAP	Me	Z	Resolution
Clean dishes	Squeak under finger	No large food particles	Good dishwasher
Safe driving distance	One car length/ ten miles per hour	One wiper width/ten miles per hour	I drive in traffic.
Quality time	Cozy coffee	Mixing cement	Date night
Healthy eating	Five a day	Meat meet meat	His 'n' hers meals
Bath comfort	Clean bath	Indoor plumbing	His 'n' hers baths
Clothes storage	Shelves and hangers	Piles	His 'n' hers closets

If you see a pattern forming here, you're on to something. Here I share another secret that Z shared with me. Back when I had all that oxytocin rolling around, I found nothing as desirable as cohabitation—the old nesting instinct. I had shoveled Z's closets and kitchen cabinets, scrubbed his bath, and scoped my corners out, and I was ready for the big move. It was then that he threw a bucket of cold water on me and said, "There's *nothing sexy* about living together." Actually the word he used was *romantic*, but I think *sexy* is more succinct.

When first he said it, I was shocked. In thirty years of living with someone, no one had ever pointed that out to me. But once he said it, I started noticing all kinds of evidence—like when you buy a Camry and all of a sudden everyone is driving one.

Here are just a few things I have since noted that fall into the "nothing sexy" category: morning mouth, indigestion, extended parental conversations, laundry, bronchitis associated with a cold or the flu, arthritic effects of climate change, large boxes of memorabilia from former lives, stained casual wear, snoring, empty coffeepots, occupied parking spaces, alarm clocks, annoying family members, socks, annoying pets, refrigerated experiments in shelf life, cranky children, crumpled Kleenex, unflushed toilets, poison ivy, the temptation to use their toothbrush to scrub said unflushed toilet, gargling—and this is the short list.

Also, in an earlier chapter, I told you about the law of attraction, which states if you truly *believe* something will happen, it is probably going to happen. Here I reveal that there is a second law of attraction. This is a law that applies specifically to cohabitation. The second law of attraction states that if two mates are within the same 2,500 square feet, they will gravitate to the same two square feet. The forces of the second law are strongest around sinks, doorways, coffeepots, couches, remote controls, and patio furniture. The danger of collision is high, so avoid hot liquids and sharp objects in second-law areas. Assigned seating resolves some of the danger, but separate living quarters is the only full resolution.

This leads me to the final bastion of male solitude: the man cave. In olden times, we had the parlor, where women gathered to do silly things like gossip and knit, while men retreated to the library to puff big cigars and discuss big politics and other dumb notions. As the family moved toward suburban ranch houses, women claimed their rightful space (the whole house), while the garage or workshop out back became the sanctuary reserved for men. Now, with the growing popularity of the modern man cave, we are experiencing a full renaissance of Cro-Magnon man.

While I often take issue with relationship expert John Gray's opinion on the gender gap, he made one observation I can personally relate to.

He said, "Men are like rubber bands." Now, I could argue, "But so are women!" After all, I myself have, at least a hundred times, pulled away only to come snapping back. However, my in-depth studies of both men and rubber bands reveal that tensile strength and ultimate elongation properties (the pressure they can take and how far they can stretch before snapping) make men much more rubber-band-like than women. This also explains the need for the man cave, which is where men go just before reaching their ultimate elongation.

And as a closing snapshot of the gender gap, I will share an event with you that is near though not very dear to me at this moment. Last night being December 21, 2012, Z and I attended an apocalypse party. In honor of our impending doom, our host produced his most ancient vintage wines and we, being the good guests we were, joyously consumed them. Now it is just past 4:00 a.m. and Z is contentedly asleep while I jot down a few postapocalyptic observations on relationships to share with you, dear reader.

You see (or, rather, hear), Z is snoring. Though I know that I, along with most of my female counterparts, occasionally emit nocturnal noise, Z is now snoring at a sustained ninety-five decibels, or roughly the volume of a jackhammer. If I knew what kind of creature a woolly mammoth might be afraid of, I believe that creature would emit this sound. And to keep things from becoming too hypnotic, occasionally Z pauses for a moment before emitting a sudden blast that, approaching 165 decibels, could be mistaken for a gunshot by our neighbors.

Z and I have a routine in which I nudge him awake and he asks, "Oh, was I snoring?" I reply, "No, dear, but I believe someone is chain-sawing their way through our front door." Z will then sleep quietly for five to seven minutes before hitting his next 165-decibel burst. The number of times we repeat this cycle on any given night varies, but tonight I have chosen to let him roar away while I entertain myself writing to you. I know I could get him one of those little plastic devices for his nose, but then I'd have that to add to the "nothing sexy" list.

CHAPTER 6

THE SECRET GARDEN

Show me your garden, and I shall tell you what you are.
—Alfred Austin

Once you have your TKT list committed to memory, it's time to put it into practice. Please take the list in your left hand, raise your right hand, and repeat after me: "I will be myself. I will be myself. I will be myself."

Now, if possible, ask your mate to do the same—with *their* list, not yours. You can go to a different room if you think this exercise is going to land on the "nothing sexy" list. This exercise should be repeated on a regular basis until you can confirm, without a doubt, that you both are honoring your TKTs. This is where the rubber meets the road, as they say in the fascinating world of elastomeric polymers.

If, however, you are still early in a relationship and between shots of oxytocin and vasopressin you happen to notice a few itty-bitty things that you think your mate should work on, I have one word for you: *Fuhgeddaboudit.* Consider yourself lucky if you get your partner to change his or her underwear. There is one thing about human nature you can take to the bank: people change only if and when *they want to.*

Now, that is not to say that you can't ask someone to change and/or provide the stimulus and reward to encourage it. In my vast experience with an extensive adult labor force, I was only mildly successful at implementing basic change by request—like asking them not to spit tobacco in the factory hallways. I found greater success after implementing the spit-and-you're-fired campaign. The operative word here—*fired*—obviously implied something to those spitters that they did not *want* to be.

So, taking this back to you and your mate, at some point during your three-year forced waiting period (go ahead, call me the relationship Nazi), you should make an itty-bitty list—yes, another one—of those itty-bitty changes you'd like to see in your mate. Then study it very hard and mark an *x* next to those things you are absolutely certain that, over time, will drive you stark raving mad. Then, very carefully, fold the list in half, fold it again in the other direction, blow on it, click your heels three times, tear it into the smallest pieces you can, and toss them aloft, laughing maniacally as they flutter down like snowflakes over your silly head.

Seriously, though, there is really nothing much you can do to change people. They have to change themselves. And therein lies the secret in this chapter: getting an important change to be *their* idea. I really shouldn't be writing this down, as Z might get around to reading it someday, but this is a risk I take to share my secret garden technique with you. I have had some early success in my secret garden, but it involves a *lot* of patience.

My secret garden technique works like this.

1. Till the ground. "Don't you think this garage is a wonderful space? It has a nice, high ceiling and such good energy!"

2. Add fertilizer. "You have so many cool and interesting tools. Don't you think they'd look like art if they were all lined up on the walls and shelves?"

3. Plant the seed. "Just look at this beautiful silverware drawer, those spoons all nested and cozy. That perfect order is so lovely it makes me want to set the table. How about a nice meaty dinner?"

4. Nurture the sprout. "This is truly turning into one of the greatest garages of all time. I can't wait to see how it looks when you're done!"

5. Water regularly. "Can I help you move in those boxes?"

6. Fertilize often. "Can I help you arrange all your beautiful tools?" (Of course, we already know the answer to this BS question.)

7. Remove weeds. Use extreme caution when performing this covert operation. Sometimes that unidentified object you are about to weed out is the one and only magneto armature remaining on the continent that will fix your lawnmower.

8. Harvest. I am still awaiting this stage, but I am happy to report the crop is coming along just fine, and I expect a bountiful harvest (i.e., an organized garage) come fall.

The length of time and the order of steps in the secret garden should be adjusted depending upon the desired harvest and your environment. If you are going for major growth, don't expect that sprout to climb to the sky right away. If you're in a drought, you must water more frequently. If a pesky varmint like habit or stubbornness nips your sprout, you may have to plant it again and again. Sometimes you have to plant lots of seeds to get just that one treasured sprout. And sometimes the garden needs *lots* of fertilizer.

Persistence is important, and patience more so, but the main key here is that *nowhere* in any of the stages does it become *your* garden. Your mate is the master gardener, and you must allow his or her garden to grow at its own pace. No matter how many hours I spend in search of a compact fluorescent light bulb, I never allow myself to scream, "Can't you get this s—organized so I can find just one freakin' bulb?!" Instead I wait for a moment when Z is most engulfed in a favorite activity and then quietly ask him for a light bulb. He stops what he is doing, retrieves one, and I coo, "Thank you, dear. If you'll show me where they are, I won't have to bother you next time."

Another thing to know about the secret garden is that you should only try to grow plants that you *really* cannot live without. The secret garden requires time, energy, and patience. And even after you have invested all of those, there's no guarantee. This is a garden that's highly susceptible to failure. So choose those crops wisely.

CHAPTER 7

BAGGAGE CHECK

Much like the garage, the bonding of two mates comes with a whole lot of baggage—emotional, psychological, and real live bags and boxes and crates and storage containers that weigh up to seven thousand pounds. Where is all that baggage gonna fit?

Of course, the heaviest of all is the emotional baggage. And if you think for one minute that you don't come with a hefty load yourself, think again. Even kids of perfect parents grow up toting around a nicely jaded set of Louis Vuittons. Remember Philosopher Mark and the lesson he shared about the purpose of parents? We all got an A in that lesson.

This brings me to an exercise I call Baggage Check. This little breather is triggered by your own sudden awareness that your mate has actually brought along a load of his or her own baggage, and requires that, before you begin to inspect your mate's, you send your own bags through the moral equivalent of airport security. Here, you take off your jacket, your shoes, and your jewelry, place your feet on the footprints, hold your hands over your head in the surrender position, and allow

Baggage Check to thoroughly scan and identify those hidden flaws in your character.

Got an addiction? Baggage Check will find those liquids and gels and contraband. Got a bad temper? Be prepared to have your bags scanned for explosives. The only difference here is that you or someone you trust (besides your mate) *is* airport security and is tasked with uncovering those hidden bombs set to blow up your relationship.

Once you have them out in full view on that long metal table, you can no longer deny them. You must realize that, even if your mom neatly packed them in there for you, they are now yours to claim. She is not the one getting busted here. Neither is your mean older brother or that previous mate who left the big hole you have since rigged with dynamite. This is time for you to own up and take responsibility for the bags that have your name and your name only on the tags. You must tell the truth. They have been in your possession the whole time.

It's your choice. You can keep those bags packed up and turn around and go home, or you can open up, throw that stuff away, and proceed on through. When airport security pulls out my four ounces of one-hundred-dollars-per-ounce face cream, the only possible response is, "Oh, yes, in the name of national security, please just go ahead and toss it." I could argue that the nation would benefit if I did in fact retain my face cream, but really, it means *nothing* to me. In other words, no matter how important your secret little flaws are to you, you've got to discard those dangerous substances if you want to pass Baggage Check.

While at Baggage Check, it's time to open up and share any critical information that you may have, for whatever reason, been withholding. This includes the following:

- Finances. Your mate should have a general knowledge of your financial state, and you should know the same about your mate.

You don't have to give him or her a full set of financial statements, just a general idea of whether you are heir to the Wrigley fortune or so far in the hole you will never see daylight.

- Faith or religion. Even though airport security cannot legally ask this question, you and your mate should bend the law and find out if the two of you hold any beliefs that might prove incompatible down the road.

- Children. If you're hiding them, cough 'em up. If you don't have any, do you want to change that? You would think this critical bit of info would never be kept from a mate, but my father had a son and daughter that he didn't tell my mother about. They were nearly her age, so no wonder—but imagine her surprise when she answered the phone one day, and a grown man said, "Let me talk to Dad." I'm just sayin'—it happens.

- Medical history. If you and your mate plan to have children, you should compare family medical history. If you have a prosthetic leg and your mate doesn't know it yet, now is probably the time to tell him or her. If you are carrying a communicable disease, it is far better to forewarn your mate than to wait and hope that he or she doesn't find out the hard way—because chances are, it'll come to light.

So now that you have rid yourself of contraband and hidden explosives and disclosed your vital information, let's take a look at some day-to-day details of managing that long relationship.

CHAPTER 8

DIRTY DETAILS

If only you trust in me, love will see us through.
—Billie Holiday

Beyond having to reveal your deepest, darkest secrets as you move into a committed relationship, there are a number of life-changing decisions that must be made. Where will you live? What name will you answer to? Will you put a ring on your finger or through your nose?

Here are just a few tips I can offer from years of research and experimentation. Though at first glance many of these tips may seem more about breaking up than staying together, I have learned that establishing some early and simple boundaries relieves much pressure from the relationship. Maintaining a certain amount of anonymity and freedom can actually improve your ability to focus on the most important thing: the relationship!

My first tip involves bank accounts. I am all for maintaining separate bank accounts, even to the death. In today's age of EFTs and debit cards, there is absolutely no reason to comingle your assets like you comingle your spit. If you must share, a simple "fun money" fund should do. Other than that, I advise that each mate stay accountable and in charge of his or her own funds. If you have none, you should probably consider a career at some point—and I don't mean that of a horizontal secretary. Individual accounts also keeps the process of reconciling your bank accounts separate from reconciling your relationship if that becomes necessary.

Other assets, fixed and liquid, are a bit trickier and far more dependent upon circumstances. The obvious advice here is to consult your lawyer, but I have found it immensely more practical to sit down with your mate beforehand and ask the age-old question: "What if one of us gets run over by a beer truck?" I have yet to see this happen in an insurance commercial, but I think it's just a matter of time.

In any event, having this open conversation prior to sitting down with the attorney's clock ticking away at twenty-five-dollar-per-minute is far more economical than the typical scenario: your attorney takes copious notes during your hour-long meeting, and five weeks later you receive an e-mail from his assistant asking for the very same information again, along with an invoice for $2,000: sixty minutes at twenty-five dollars per minute, plus $500 for incidentals (coffee, water, pen, paper).

If children are involved—yours, theirs, or both—or if you plan to have children, the beer truck discussion is mandatory.

Next, let's discuss the forever name change. As a female, the key thing to remember here is this: the postman never forgets. Despite your best intentions right now, there are not many downers so bad as going to the mailbox for the rest of your life to be reminded of who you used to be. If you really like your present name, you might want to keep it—or at least hyphenate it. If you voice this option to your mate and get a truly negative reaction, you might want run that bag through the scanner one more time. It's not necessarily a deal breaker, but you should understand what's in there.

In deciding on last names, cultural norms should be taken into account. In some parts of the South, you might find a red letter around your neck when you check into the Holiday Inn under different names. If you are Japanese and your wife's family is more prosperous than yours, then you get to take her family name on. And, of course, children play heavily in the decision. If you plan to have children together, one last name for all saves a lot of explaining and monogramming. However, if you are female and have children from a previous relationship, you might want to consider keeping that old bag of a name at least until they reach college age. Changing your name without a marriage license costs about $150 and a post in the newspaper. So if you want, you can take your time to ponder this one.

The rings—those eternal and endless symbols of love—must be chosen with great care and deep financial commitment, or not. Now, don't get me wrong here. I love rings. I love the way they feel and the way they look and the endless promises they symbolize. I love the ceremony that accompanies their placement. I firmly believe it to be a wonderful custom. But I don't wear one and doubt I ever will. In the spirit of Baggage Check, I'll reveal to you a deep, dark secret of mine.

I have, in my past, had recurring ring dreams. Usually they ended with me waking in a panic, searching for a precious ring I lost in the dream. The most terrifying had me choking on the ring, a dream I frequently had during a troubled engagement. It's a good thing rings are round and open, because one night I awoke to find the ring actually lodged in the back of my throat. If I'd swallowed it, it would've been an ordeal of epic proportion. Happily, that never came to pass. Nor did the wedding.

Now, any good dream interpreter would say I have an issue with commitment, and I would have to agree that he or she is a very good dream interpreter. At one point, I considered tattooing "LTR" with a big circle and an *x* on my forearm. After some serious relationship failures, it took me years of U TIME to overcome my fears and trust in my mate—and, more importantly, in myself.

Z also chose to avoid the wedding ring route, so now we just stroll around barehanded, most of the time holding hands. His reason is the danger of getting the ring hooked on one of his copious tools. My reason is also safety related—I just don't want to choke on it in my sleep.

As a final dirty detail, I recently read of a correlation between money spent on a wedding and the relationship's chance of failure—as in the more money spent, the greater the chance of failure. While I have not been able to statistically verify this, I thought passing it along might save you some money. Also, for undocumented reasons, ice sculptures at the reception are a sure sign of doom. I hold no statistical support for this tidbit either, but do recall a lovely ice fish holding a bowl of crab dip in its mouth at my second wedding.

So there no right answers and no wrong ones in this chapter—just a few things to consider as you move forward into that long relationship. The main point to take away here is that you should keep things as simple as possible. Simple decisions allow you to focus on the one and only most important thing right now: a wonderful and continuously improving relationship between you and your mate.

CHAPTER 9

EVERY PARTNER HAS
A PURPOSE

Sometimes it takes a good fall to really know where you stand.
—Hayley Williams

The road to finding that perfect partner can be as painful as childbirth, if you have experience with that. If not, maybe slam your hand in the car door several times to get the rough equivalent. So what do you do when the country music begins to play and you find yourselves two-stepping toward separate exits?

Face it—breakups happen. Entire musical genres have been launched off the backs of failed relationships. Many, many yachts and second homes and BMWs have been purchased with the funds required to unravel them. Entire religions and empires have been founded on less.

So what advice can I possibly offer on the direction of the exit door and how fast it's approaching? Let's see. How about some signs that the end is nigh?

- when you begin to mentally separate your belongings
- when you begin to physically separate your belongings stored in out-of-the-way spots, such as under the bathroom sink
- when you call the moving truck
- when you say things to your mate in his or her absence that you don't say to his or her face
- when you have *the talk*
- when these words cross your lips face-to-face: "I can't live like this anymore"
- when your heart no longer races when you hear your mate at the door
- when you hang up the phone when you hear him or her at the door
- when you run to the door and lock it

Now, I am not an advocate of quickly throwing in the towel. I am all for giving a relationship all you got, particularly if you have advanced through the stages and reached the commitment stage. If you have children together, there is no good time or way to split up, but there are times and ways you can research that may inflict a lesser amount of pain and damage on them. But face it, there are times when throwing in the towel is really just the least bad of many bad options.

With no easy way to say good-bye, the most common breakup line is "It's not you; it's me. I just need some space." If you hear that more than once and time proves that it's not just your mate rubber banding, don't expect the relationship to continue. If you say that and it's not just you rubber-banding, don't expect them to understand right away. Often you have to repeat it well into the hundreds of times before they hear what you are really saying: "Let me *outta here!*" If you hear it from several mates in sequence, I suggest you go back to Baggage Check and run through the scanner a few more times.

So when it comes time to go, try not to whine and whimper too much. Turn off that country music station. Don't just stand there and allow yourself or your mate to suffer death by a thousand cuts. Pull off the Band-Aid as quick as you can. Rip off that rearview mirror. Start back on page one, get your U TIME clock ticking, and get yourself ready to give it another go!

That's oversimplified, I know, but in all actuality, no matter which side of the severing knife you are on or what advice you get, you are going to deal with the pain of a split on your own terms and conditions. All I can really offer to fill that deep black hole of breakup pain are some diversionary and/or affirmative ideas that might get your heart pumping again. So here are my fill-the-black-hole suggestions.

- The breakup diet: Celebrate the weight loss that accompanies your natural loss of appetite during devastating emotional trauma. Go out and buy some new jeans—or heck, buy an entire wardrobe that you pick out just for yourself.

- The single-and-lovin'-it tour: Call your most adventuresome friend(s) and book a trip ASAP to the most adventuresome place you can afford. It can be a weekend or a month. Just do it quick and fill it with fun. No waiting, period.

- Move: I know this is drastic, but sometimes, particularly if you lived in a small community, it may be the one thing that allows you to breathe again. Not only will you surround yourself with new faces and places, a move lets a new and improved you emerge from the dust and rubble. Just run those bags through Baggage Check to see which ones to leave behind.

Since all of the above involve money, here are a few more ideas I'll throw in for the thrifty among us.

- Write a book, journal, poem, or song about the relationship. You don't have to publish it or share it with anyone. It is just for you. In fact, once you have it finished, you may want to build a bonfire and ceremonially torch it. However, if you do share it, you may relish the royalties that result from your painful artistic endeavor. Taylor Swift seems to have made a highly lucrative career out of this.

- Volunteer to do something you've never done before. While you are giving your time for the general improvement of something or someone, you will find that in return you receive new acquaintances and new experiences as a reward, not to mention possible tax deductions.

- Take a free online college class. There are now some amazing opportunities to learn out there just by searching the Internet. Try Physics and Chemistry of Terrestrial Planets at MIT or History of the World since 1300 at Princeton. The choices are growing and amazingly interesting. Along the way, you might find yourself with a new degree, a new career, and an extra zero or two on your W-2.

- Refer back to the first U TIME exercise—pruning deadwood—and clean out *x*. *X* can be any or all of the rooms in your dwelling, the back seat of your car, or even your backpack. Once you are done, not only will you have a clean *x* and a feeling of accomplishment, you will probably find the phone number or e-mail for that really adorable person you almost reached out to just before you met your ex-mate.

- Get back in touch with those true friends you left behind while you were spending all that time with your ex-mate. They are all still out there on Facebook or the other end of the phone, waiting to hear what's up in your life.

One note of caution during this fragile pick-yourself-up-and-dust-yourself-off period: avoid people who bring you down or find pleasure in your pain. There are those among us who are sworn to celibacy, usually as a result of some deep, dark pain they have stored out back in a heavily guarded, armored truck. That's okay, but some take it to an extreme and believe that everyone else should join them in their celibacy. Not only are they a danger to the future of life on the planet, but just being around them is a real bummer as well.

If you look out back and see your own armored truck but are reading this book, I am guessing you hold out a candle for love, however dim and wasting. Let me say there's hope for you. Just grab the keys to that truck, go open the damned thing up, and run everything in there through Baggage Check. Whatever horrors someone has put you through and left you with, try your best to get rid of them. Otherwise, they will mildew and stink up the place—or, worse still, self-ignite over time.

My advice is to open them up, look them over real hard one last time, remove your name tags, and toss them out in the street on garbage day. To whoever left you with that garbage, thumb your nose. The best revenge is a good life, and a good life does not include pain and self-pity.

Whether you or your mate has initiated the ending, remember that every partner has a purpose. Sometimes it completes your what-I-don't-want list. Sometimes it prepares you for that perfect partner to come. I think if Z and I had met thirty years ago, we would have probably looked right past each other. He would have been too edgy for me, and I was far too career-oriented for him. It took decades of evolving for us to get ready for each other. And for that we have to thank all the ones we've loved (and been hurt by) before.

While we're thanking people, let's not forget a shout-out to those exes. For some reason that I really do not understand, we are trained to look disdainfully upon the former mates of our own mate. They are often viewed as some kind of abstract competition, to which I say, "Really?" Unless your mate is or was a cheater, in which case they should be denied the time of day anyway, there is no direct link between yourself and your mate's former choice. As the reigning senior partner here, you may choose to relate to the ex-mates however you deem appropriate.

For myself, I have to give thanks to Z's ex-wives club. Though neither of his exes made his life a walk in the park, they obviously gave him firsthand experience in how to choose his battles. And they schooled him on when to turn off that flamethrower of his and instead use the two-word fire extinguisher known as "Yes, dear." To you ladies, I owe much for your hard years of service. You have indeed lowered the odds that I will ever have to join your club.

So whatever state you find yourself in after a breakup, which in my experience ranges from suicidal to sheer elation, just remember that it is temporary, without a shadow of a doubt. Just like little orphan Annie says, the sun will come out tomorrow. You *will* see your way out of the fog. You *must* let go of the pain, as you are now one step closer to finding that perfect partner. The sooner you let go, the sooner you can grasp the next. It's that old law of attraction again. Believe and you will see.

CHAPTER 10

CELEBRATE!

Against all odds, honey, we're the big door prize.
—John Prine

W*oo-hoo!* You've arrived at chapter 10! This one packs a real party, and rightfully so. You've come a long way, baby. It's time to get down and *celebrate*! If you and your partner followed the rules and guidelines and reach this stage of commitment, you should party at every drop of the hat. But just so you don't get too carried away, think of these parties as baby showers and your relationship as a newborn baby.

You have to feed it, and you have to dress it. You have to say kinds words and give it hugs and put it down for naps now and then. Sometimes you have to burp it and occasionally change a smelly diaper. As you care for it, it will grow healthy bones and teeth and a bright smile. It might even make all As and go on to get a scholarship to an Ivy League school and eventually document the key to quantum physics. Okay, I'm getting carried away again—but aren't relationships every bit as puzzling as quantum physics?

There are *so* many ways to nurture your baby. My personal favorite is date night—a predetermined date, greatly anticipated but with no set schedule, when Z and I get a room at a hot springs and a couple of massages and enjoy a bottle of wine, a great meal, and each other. Sometimes we even end up dancing in the street. For you and your mate, it can be anything that appeals to the *both* of you. Keep on experimenting; the whole process of figuring it out can become great fun.

If you are looking for some simple ideas to get started, you might try taking dance lessons, reading to each other, or spending an afternoon getting coffee or tea with a nice dessert—just as long as it appeals to *both* of you. The easiest place to start is with something you both enjoyed back in the romance stage. It doesn't need to be expensive, just ritual. We have friends who celebrate weekends like this: she opens beer bottles with her belly button, and he tells bawdy jokes. Not exactly my cup of tea, but hey, it works.

One thing I have found common to most long relationships is some form of eating ritual. It does not necessarily involve food preparation, though most often it does. Most foodies I know are coupled up and deeply in love with their recipes, their wine selections, and each other. But even if the only thing you make is reservations, you can still develop a delightful eating ritual.

Keeping up appearances will nurture your baby, especially since over time you will start to look like each other—*really!* And the more sex you have, the more oxytocin and vasopressin you produce, and the more you will idealize that person who now begins to look more like you with every passing year. Your love life is a great reason to stay in shape, though every year this gets harder. Fortunately, as your body ages, so does your eyesight. This is when idealization *really* comes in handy.

Conversation is big. It doesn't have to be many words, just the right kind at the right time. Some great mates go days on just a few grunts, while others keep a constant running dialogue. This can change over time and circumstances. I know this for a fact because my first conversation with Z lasted fourteen hours. I was on my cell phone back in the days of roaming, and it cost me $792—officially my most expensive first date *ever*. Now when we're apart, a fourteen-minute chat every now and then is plenty, even with unlimited minutes. That's okay, because when we get back together again, there's always *lots* to talk about. I once heard Hillary Clinton say, "Bill and I started a conversation in 1971, and it's still going on." Now, I am guessing parts of that chat were a bit more animated than others, but *that's* a sign of a long relationship.

Dr. John Huston, our aforementioned Texas researcher who spent fourteen years keeping tabs on 168 couples, has identified three things in common that satisfied couples give each other. And no, it's not diamond earrings, a Maserati, and an orgasm. Dr. Huston found that of all the things a couple can give each other, the most effective are warmth, kindness, and concern. Remember these, as they are simple but golden: warmth, kindness, concern. I have experimented extensively with them and learned that all three are available on demand, in public or private, and with a credit score well under eight hundred.

Before we leave this party known as chapter 10, bear with me as I assign you one final list: a list of buttons. You know those red ones you push to fire off your mate's nuclear reactor? Yeah, you do—they have something to do with family, history, habits, friends, or career (read: *money*.) Those damned little gadgets should have been confiscated in Baggage Check, but somehow they made it through the scanner.

Okay, now write them down. Think about it. Make sure you got 'em all. Then recite this list and commit it to permanent memory. Once you have it forever emblazoned on your brain, shred that list, and never, *ever* push those buttons again. Got it? Not *ever*—even if you are in one of your blackest burn-the-house-down moods. Just think of it this way: every time you push a red button, that little baby of yours takes the hit.

My street research team tells me a key to a long relationship is to not go to bed mad. I take this to mean to let a fight go quick, especially since I find myself sleeping in the guest bedroom at least two nights a year. The equation here is that a short fight leads to less damage. In other words, don't stay mad any longer than you can stay awake.

So there you have it—you and your big door prize! And this time around you are fully trained and licensed to possess it, concealed or not. So go right ahead and stuff that pistol in your pocket, get behind that wheel, and head out on a road trip with the prize of your life. The real prize is that the road goes on forever, and the party never ends. At least that's what we're after here.

CHAPTER 11

THE DUPLICATE KEY RULE

Love is not a victory march. It's a cold and it's a broken hallelujah.
—*Leonard Cohen*

Think of this as your bonus round. Chapter 11 is not so much about relationships as your individual quest for sustained happiness. And if you can contribute just one thing to a long relationship, happiness is the equivalent of massive doses of steroids. Z refers to it as the "happy gene," but I believe it can be a learned attribute. Happiness is a premium option that costs you absolutely nothing. And it comes with more benefits than a job at Starbucks.

The happiest person I ever knew distilled his method down to three steps:

1. Have something to do.
2. Have something to look forward to.
3. Have someone to share it with.

Number three, of course, is what this book is all about. But please realize that the someone you share it with does not have to be your mate. It can be friends, family, or folks at work—anyone in your circle or many in your circle. The operative word here is *share*. The things to do and to look forward to are entirely up to you.

To this small list of steps, I must add a fourth: respect your karma. Good and bad events roll in and out like the tide, sometimes with the force of a category-five hurricane. We may never know why, but it seems to happen this way—when you do good, good things happen to you; when you do bad, you'll get it back someday.

A recent poster child for karma neglect is the formerly venerated cyclist Lance Armstrong. It would seem that, besides breaking many professional cycling rules and guidelines, Lance took some people down in a nasty fashion along the way. As usual, karma finally caught up with him. And here I must add a little-known chapter to his monumental descent from glory.

In the mid-1980s, my sister conceived of and gave birth to a remarkable new product: a rubber-band bracelet with an imprinted message. Yet this opportunity for fame and fortune was upended, unfortunately for her, by a certain yellow rubber-band bracelet produced for a mere fraction of the cost in Asia. While I am in no way a protectionist—I drive a Toyota and, like most Americans, dress mostly in Honduran- and Turkish-made attire, I do believe that if that particular yellow bracelet had been made at a certain rubber band factory I know of, many skilled Americans would have benefited and purchased many US-made yellow bracelets for one dollar a piece.

Who knows? My sister might have even enjoyed her own Tour de France. Instead, she now clocks roughly ninety miles a week down the corridors of a certain factory, while that Asian yellow bracelet and its US nonprofit organization have amassed a fortune of over $100 million.[8] Forgive me if I've missed something here, but I see nothing nonprofit about that. Regardless, Lance was destined to teach us his own lesson about karma: what goes around comes around, just like those two wheels that rode him straight past glory wearing that little yellow bracelet of his.

So now we come upon the Duplicate Key Rule. Like everything else in this book, the Duplicate Key Rule is very simple. It only requires this: that you always keep at least one copy of your own key to happiness. Never, not ever, *not no way, not no how* give anyone or anything your *only* key.

You see, all people and all things have a finite shelf life. Intentionally or not, they can and do expire. And that event is often completely out of your control. If something or someone other than you has that only key, you will find yourself locked out—and not on some balmy afternoon. When it happens, it will usually be in a driving blizzard with wind gusts of up to fifty miles per hour.

So, if you must give away a key to your happiness, just please, *please* be sure you have a duplicate hidden away somewhere for yourself. Try it out to make sure it works—now, before you find yourself standing in that blizzard. And if somewhere, on some dark and rainy night, someone tries to slip you their only key, do them (and yourself) a big favor. Make yourself a copy and give it back.

SUMMARY

S o there you have it—the short guide to helping you achieve and sustain that long and wonderful relationship. The rules, guidelines, and exercises in this book make a logical leap past the follow-your-heart-but-keep-your-fingers-crossed method that brought us a 50 percent divorce rate. Knowing yourself is big. Taking the time to get to know your mate is even bigger. And accepting your mate for what he or she is is the home run of relationships.

This is a lifelong journey, so you might want to keep this short guide around awhile. You can use it for a plant stand in the meantime—but please, not if it's an e-book. If it's hardcopy, you might find it to be like any favorite old book: the best parts get more worn than others, and the book just falls open to them. I miss that feature on my e-reader.

And this book holds a guarantee: if you ever see the Z and me divorce trending on the Internet, you can return this book for full credit toward my next release: *Loner 101: A Short Guide to Avoiding Relationships Altogether*. In the meantime, log onto love101book.com and let me know how it's going.

APPENDIX

This section contains a reference chart, tear-out lists, and your very own certificate of achievement for completing LOVE101. Note: if this is an e-book, please *do not* attempt to tear them out. You can download and print hardcopies at www. love101book.com.

U TIME Handy Reference Chart		
F TIME		U TIME
More Than	*But Less Than*	
—	One year	A month or so
One year	Two years	A few months
Two years	Four years	Six months to a year
Four years	Eight years	One to two years
Eight years	Twelve years	Two to three years
Twelve years	Sixteen years	Three to four Years
Sixteen years	Twenty years	Four to five Years
Twenty years	—	Heck, go for it!

To Know Thyself (TKT) List

Brainstorm and prioritize the aspects of life that bring you most happiness, or alternatively, document those things that you are most unhappy without. Examples include travel, fine cuisine, books, my cat, fashion, shotguns, and the color yellow.

Brainstorm	Order of Importance	Comments

Painting My Perfect Partner		
Characteristic	**Check One**	
	Want	*Don't Want*

If you are so inclined, please feel free to create a visual instead.

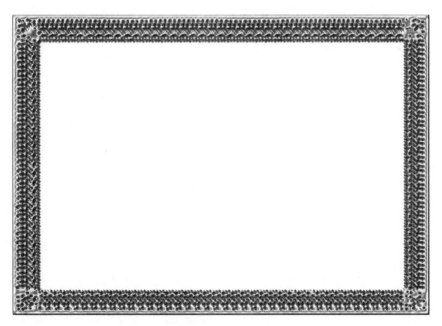

My Perfect Partner

Past Relationship Case Study (Copy as required.)		
Case Number		Duration
Notes		
Occupation		
Physical Characteristics		
Pros		
Cons		
Fault Signal One		
Rationalization One		
Fault Signal Two		
Rationalization Two		
Seminal Romantic Moment		
Intensity		
Living Arrangement		
Critical Fail Signals		
Attempted Resolution		
Result And Analysis		

Red Button List

Make a list of red buttons that set off your mate's nuclear reactor.

Then commit this list to memory, tear it up, and *never* touch those buttons again.

Button Number/Location	Description

Note: If more than seven spaces are needed, professional help is advised.

LOVE 101
Certificate of Achievement

BE IT HEREBY CERTIFIED THAT

_____

HAS PURSUED THE COURSES OF
STUDY PRESCRIBED IN LOVE 101
AND HAS SATISFIED THE STATU-
TORY REQUIREMENTS AND YOUR
OWN CONSCIENCE THAT YOU ARE,
INDEED AND AT LAST, ARMED
WITH THE NECESSARY INFORMA-
TION TO EMBARK UPON A LONG
RELATIONSHIP. YOU ARE NOW AD-
MITTED TO AN UNDETERMINED
DEGREE OF LOVE FOR AN UNDE-
TERMINED PERIOD WITH ALL THE
RIGHTS, PRIVILEGES AND DUTIES
ATTENDANT THERETO.*

*Current conditions are no guarantee of future results. Void where prohibited by law or tribal custom. Neither author, publisher or bookseller assume legal responsibility for usefulness of this certificate. Prolonged relationship exposure may be associated with rashes, indigestion, unexplained feelings of elation or anxiety, sleeplessness and hair loss. Consult your physician if any of these symptoms persist more than three weeks. Consult your attorney if symptoms persist more than three years.

NOTES

1. *Wikipedia*, s.v. "Law of attraction," last modified June 11, 2013, http://en.wikipedia.org/wiki/Law_of_attraction.
2. *Wikipedia*, s.v. "Falling in love," last modified May 19, 2013, http://en.wikipedia.org/wiki/Falling_in_love.
3. John Money, *Lovemaps: Clinical Concepts of Sexual/Erotic Health and Pothology, Paraphilia and Gender Transposition of Childhood, Adolescence, and Maturity* (New York: Irvington Publishers, 1986).
4. Lisa Diamond, "Emerging Perspectives on Distinctions Between Romantic Love and Sexual Desire," *Current Directions in Psychological Science* (June 2004): 116-119.
5. Larry Young and Brian Alexander, *The Chemistry Between Us: Love, Sex and the Science of Attraction* (New York: Penguin, 2012).
6. Kay Randall, "What's Love Got to Do With It?" last modified February 10, 2003, The University of Texas at Austin, accessed December 15, 2012, http://www.utexas.edu/features/archive/2003/love.html.
7. *Wikipedia*, s.v. "Sex (disambiguation)," last modified May 19, 2013, http://en.wikipedia.org/wiki/Sex_disambiguation.
8. "Financial Information," Livestrong Foundation, accessed June 4, 2013, http://www.livestrong.org/Who-We-Are/Our-Strength/Financial-Information.

CPSIA information can be obtained at www.ICGtesting.com
Printed in the USA
BVOW04s2047170913

331444BV00001B/16/P